MW01025771

# CHOSEN

# ON

# PURPOSE

*A Series of Divine Encounters*

**By Ronald J. Dempsey**

**CEDAR GATE**
**PUBLISHING**

# DEDICATION

I dedicate this book to my parents
Patrick & Jane Dempsey
...and to
David Kennedy, Brian Hughes and
Dr. Angus MacDonald (My bagpipe teachers)

# Table of Contents

# Foreword:

I wanted to take the time to drop Ronald a line to say thank you for talking with me that day in the laundromat about having faith enough in God to know that nothing is impossible.

On that morning I wasn't just thinking about suicide, I had actually bought the shotgun and shells to blow my head off!! I believe God Himself put Ronald in the perfect position that day to intercede.

I read every word of his book Chosen on Purpose... I know from personal experience Ronald Dempsey is truly one of His Chosen.


May God bless you as he has blessed me!!!

Mary

# Introduction:

**O**ver the years, countless people, having heard me give parts of my testimony, have commented to me they felt I needed to write this book. In doing so, my testimony might reach the entire world and maybe strengthen the faith of fellow Christians, believers and non-believers of the world. So here I wish to share my experiences with God. Having had Jesus call me by name and walk me through the narrow gate of salvation, I was then led with no doubt to do God's will.

Let me say that I am a born-again Christian, soldier, and servant of the Lord Jesus Christ, my Father, and the Holy Spirit. And, like the rest of the world, I am imperfect and a sinner. I have been saved by grace and sealed in the Holy Spirit.

I realize this project could consist of writing several books to cover everything I have experienced. This could be a massive undertaking which could take the rest of my life to complete. Every time I testify it is like living the experience all over again; the tears from the emotion I felt at the time always flow. The presence of the Holy Spirit with His intense love is so overwhelming to me I can't seem to be able to hold back the tears.

There have been times I wondered (or maybe Satan was trying to make me doubt) . . . did I really experience these things, or did I imagine them? If I imagined them, or at least my part in them, then how and why did the rest of it, which I had no control over, also happen? And why do the others involved have similar stories about how they knew to do what they did at the same time?

# Encounter

*Number One*

## *A Daily Word from Curtis!*

I sometimes think about where it really began for me. I wonder if it was Mrs. Booth, who used to babysit for us when we were kids. She must have been over 100 years old, and she was always reading her Bible. Or was it in high school with the black janitors, Willie, Jess, Fred and Curtis, who always had a new verse to quote for the day? We would see Curtis and ask, "What is the Word for the day, Curtis?" He would then quote a verse from scripture. I think the other catholic boys did it in jest, but I listened.

**I** was raised Roman Catholic. My parents were wonderful, strict parents who loved us and cared for us. But as Catholics, we weren't pushed to read the Bible. It was my sophomore year in high school when I realized the Roman Catholic Doctrine is not the whole truth. So, I began my life-long search for the absolute truth. "Seek and ye shall find, knock and the door will be opened unto you." (Matthew 7:7)

**I** will inject here that I realize as I am writing this how controversial my opinion will become; I'm sure many "religions" will take affront to what I am saying. However, in reading scripture, God Himself does say that "religion" is meaningless. If we have the need to practice religion, scripture says to care for His widows and orphans, to love Him and one another. To not kill or steal, to not bear false witness, to not worship any God but Him, etc. But, essentially, what I am saying is that God has nothing to do with "religion" and "religion" has nothing to do with God!

**I**n my experience most churches are just businesses aimed at making money and offer, at best, a watered-down version of the truth. They are the money changers that Jesus kicked out of the temple. To me the ultimate "bottom line" and the only one that really matters (whether you believe it or not) is that one day you will face the Almighty God. Hopefully for everyone reading this, He says, "Welcome home my good and faithful servant!"

**B**ut reality dictates that unlike the opinion of a certain female talk show host, there is only one way to get to heaven, and that is through Jesus Christ – not Buddha, not Mohammed, not Joe Smith and all the others. That is just people getting it wrong and wasting their time. Yes, the

Mormons and Buddhists and Muslims have it all wrong.

**I** have seen Christian teenagers going on mission trips to Russia. They collect all the money they need for airfare, lodging and food beforehand. They don't know the customs of the Russian people or speak their language. When asked how long they plan to be there, it's usually one to two weeks.

**T**he reality I see is these children are not going on a mission, but on a paid vacation. If they were truly going on a mission requested by God, they would do as the apostles did. They would go with the clothes on their back, taking no provisions, and their needs would be met as (in faith) they walked it out.

**S**uch displays of false missions make me sick. That is just religiosity. Some church groups will preach that God does not speak audibly anymore, and that is a lie. God has not changed. Some people will say the Bible was written by men, but every word was inspired by God's hand.

# Encounter

*Number Two*

### My Bosses Were Preachers

**B**efore I laid down my life to God, I had been living a very sinful life. I had become a sexual addict, and I suppose just like any "addiction of choice," I knew where to go, who to see, and how to get it. Eventually I had gotten to the point where, although I was walking and alive physically, spiritually I was dead, and I knew it.

It was not uncommon for me to have sex with three women a day (not something I'm proud of). I remember looking in the mirror and not liking what I saw. I was a slut, a whore, and I saw death in my eyes. Over a ten-year period, I had been with 37 women. If given the chance, I would have gladly traded them all for just one!

Then one day, I took off my clothes, thinking it to be part of humbling myself and coming before God as when I was first born. I lay face down on the floor (which I found later was biblical-prostrate before the Lord) and said, "Lord, my way doesn't work, let's do it your way."

The very next day I went down to a local jobsite where houses were being built. I have always been fascinated by the process of building houses, and at the time I didn't even make the correlation of Jesus being a carpenter. I saw a man I thought was the foreman and asked, "Are you the foreman?"

He was. His name was Terry Ewers. I told him I didn't know how to do that kind of work but would like to learn how. I asked if he would consider hiring me as an apprentice. I even offered to work for free just to learn the trade.

Terry said, "No, you won't work for free." He paid his helpers $15.00 an hour, and that's what I'd get paid. Since his helper was leaving, I was hired on the spot. It was perfect timing and God is always involved in perfect timing.

As it turned out, Terry was also a preacher, not the church kind, but an out-among-the-people kind, like a Johnny Appleseed. I was with Terry for three months. The next guy I was put with was also a preacher, and the next, and the next, right down the line from the day I surrendered my life to the Lord.

I write this now, having bare my past sins for the world to judge. I am an open book. Don't get me wrong, I'm not saying it was all glorious and that I lived happily ever after. There were times of plenty and times of need, but the walk and adventure continued. At this point, I must say that in my experience, there is no such thing as coincidence! I always meet the people I'm supposed to. I always have, and I always will.

# Encounter

*Number Three*

## *A Woman on the Road*

As I recall, my first experience was while driving near Atlanta, Georgia. A woman was stopped by the side of a road, so I pulled over to see if I could assist in some way. Her truck wouldn't start. Being an A&P mechanic, I did everything I knew how to get it going, but it still wouldn't start.

At this point, I was angry and frustrated. Pointing at her truck, I looked up and shouted, "Get down here and start this thing!" I started to say, "I have no doubt that you can do it," but all I was able to get out of my mouth was, "I have no doubt." Right then it felt like the power of three lightning bolts came through my body, out of my arm and into her truck. It was so powerful I was literally thrown to the ground.

I remember wondering if I had any hair left. I stood up, still pointing at her truck and laughing like crazy; it must have been a comical scene. I knew at that moment that as soon as she turned the key her truck was going to fire right up and start. I just knew, no doubt in my mind. Half laughing, I said, "Try it now lady!"

She turned the key and it started right up. I told her I'd never had anything like that happen before, but I had to tell her about it. She said she already knew what had happened; while I was speaking, I was suddenly thrown to the ground, and she had been thrown up against the door. She asked, "What did you say?"

I replied, "Whatever it was, I don't think I'll say it again!"

# Encounter

*Number Four*

## *The Doll Shop*

N ext, I was driving in Covington, Georgia, when I heard a voice speak. It said, "Park your car in that parking space and go into that store." My eyes were directed to the specific places. I parked my jeep and went into the store.

I didn't see anybody, so I called out, "Is anybody here?"

It was a doll shop. I thought, I didn't know I was supposed to buy a doll. I said to myself, if there is some little girl somewhere that You want me to buy a doll for, show me which one and I'll buy it. As I looked around, I again shouted, "Is anybody here?" Still no answer. I said, "Usually You have me in a place for a reason, but since no one is here, maybe I got the wrong store. Maybe You meant next door."

I turned to go, but I saw something on the floor through the glass display case. I went to look and there was a woman on the floor. There was blood on her forehead, her cash drawer was open, and cash was spilled everywhere. I assumed she had been robbed, so I quickly called the police and the fire department. I then got on the floor to comfort her. She was unconscious but I reassured her that medically she was in good hands since I had the gift of healing; I had been a Navy Corpsman. Also, considering who had sent me to her store, she really was in good hands. The police arrived to take care of her, I made my report, and left the store.

Three days later I was shopping in the same area. The woman from the store came running out of her shop yelling, "That's him! That's the man who came to help me!"

I replied to her, "Ma'am, you were unconscious. You couldn't have known I was the man."

She answered, "It's as if you and that other guy were right there with me."

Confused since I had been alone, I asked, "What other guy?"

She said, "I'm not sure who he was, but he was very bright and beautiful!"

# Encounter

*Number Five*

## *Three Foreign Gentlemen*

Another time, a friend of mine was attending Alcoholics Anonymous, and I went to a meeting with him. This was a regional meeting with a group of over 600 people. As I listened, one guy stood up and said he was trying something, and it wasn't working; another guy said he was trying something else and it wasn't working either.

I raised my hand and introduced myself. I said that if you look at the AA Twelve-Step Program, you will come to the realization you can't do it on your own. I explained this is particularly true for the second and third steps. **But** if you turn it over to Him (the Lord), He will do it for you.

When I said those words, it's hard to describe what happened next. It was like my conscious mind was thrown into the proverbial backseat. The only thing I was aware of was that my lips were moving, but I wasn't doing the talking anymore. Words were spoken for 45 minutes and the room was so quiet, except for the speaking, you could have heard a pin drop... and it was a carpeted room.

Afterward, a man came to me and asked what had happened. I told him all I knew was it wasn't me doing the talking. He said that made sense. I asked, "Why does that make sense?"

He replied, "What you may not have known is that in the back of the room tonight, we had three gentlemen who spoke three separate languages, other than English." He explained that each gentleman had an interpreter with him. However, without the help of their interpreters, each one heard what I said in his native tongue. Knowing full well that everybody else heard it in English, they said that only God could have done that, and the man speaking was a servant of God.

Be mindful of the fact though, that even in being chosen, we are merely vessels or channels being used by Him. Everything is His doing, for His glory. Yes, it's an honor to be used, but people need to be told to praise and honor Him, not us, or me in this case.

I believe this was the true "gift of tongues" He gave to the apostles at Pentecost. The apostles spoke their own native tongue and ten people from ten different countries heard it in their language in one speaking. They would say only

God could do this, because tongues are for the unbeliever not for the believer.

When it was happening, I didn't hear what was said as I was "speaking," and it didn't register in my memory. The AA session was recorded, and afterward I was given a copy of the tape. When I listened to the recording, my voice was recorded up to the "speaking." That part was not recorded. You could hear coughing and sneezes from the audience but nothing else. I remember one man saying that he didn't need to have religion jammed down his throat, so whatever was said pertained to that.

# Encounter

*Number Six*

## A Knock on My Window

**B**efore I get into this one, let me back it up a bit. I was in Colorado following the "speaking" incident. I was told by God to go to Roundup, Montana, so I went. It was November and winter was setting in. I was driving a 1967 Pontiac LeMans that I had purchased for $300.

When I got to Roundup, I slept in a park by the river in my tent. My sleeping bag was a goose-down Bugaboo bag, good for temps to 40 degrees below zero. I slept well, but I knew I couldn't continue sleeping there; I needed to find a place to live and brought it to God's attention. I shopped all the possible leads and there wasn't even a shack to be had. The loggers had taken everything available. I told God that I had done everything He had asked of me, and if he wanted me in Roundup, He would have to provide a place for me to live. I'd already looked everywhere, so I was leaving Roundup.

While driving, my car turned into the IGA grocery store parking lot. I fought it but it seemed to have a will of its own. I thought maybe I had a flat tire, but when I got out to look, I was physically pushed into the store. I know because I resisted all the way. Once in the store, I argued with God telling Him that I had no need for groceries. I had no place to put them and I wasn't even hungry. Finally, I bought some milk and cookies just to get out of the store.

On the way out, I noticed an index card on the bulletin board that said, "Room for Rent - $100 a Month." I called the number immediately and asked if the room was still available. They told me they had just put the card on the bulletin board about eight minutes ago. I suppose if I hadn't bought the milk and cookies, I would have met them posting the ad. I now had a place to live, and it was a nice, warm, furnished room.

The next Monday, I went to Billings to look for work. The first place I went to hired me. I now had a job. It was a fifty-mile drive each way and gas was only thirty-seven cents a gallon. Five hundred miles a week seemed to be a bit much, but I endured it till summer came.

I recall one Sunday, my third Sunday in Roundup. The minister of the church I was attending told the congregation there was a family in their church group whose house, barn and out buildings had burned down the night before. They had no insurance. The pastor said, "Let's all pray for them and hope they do better."

I stood up and asked, "Isn't there a passage in Scripture that says if we have a fellow Christian in a situation like this, we're supposed to do everything we can to help them? If all we do is say, 'I hope you do better. We'll pray for you,' then where is the love of the Father in you?

"How about I throw in six months work as a carpenter," I suggested, "and someone else could provide the brick." I went on to say, "Another person could help with the plumbing, and together we could build them a new house." The Amish help their neighbors, why shouldn't we?

Summer came and while I worked in Billings, I also worked out in a gym there. Directly across from the gym was a big field full of old rusty cars. I thought maybe I could park my own rusty car among them, sleep on the front seat, and shower and shave at the gym. On Friday and Saturday, I did just that.

On Sunday, I awoke and prayed while I was still laying down. I told God that it was Sunday and asked Him to tell me what church I should attend. I knew the gym didn't open until 9:00am, so I couldn't shower and shave before church. I figured I'd just sit in the back so I wouldn't offend anyone.

Right then, there was a knock on my window. I opened my car door, and it was a man who was out walking his dog. He told me he lived in the house just down the street and noticed I had been sleeping here the last couple of nights. I thought maybe I was trespassing on someone's land and asked if I was in trouble. The man said no, but he and his wife wondered if I would like to come up to the house to shower and shave. I mentioned I was just praying about that when he knocked on the window. He then replied, "In fact, why not just move in with us!"

When my job ended in Billings, I was told there was another job I could have if I could be in Livingston, Montana by Monday morning. At the time, I didn't have enough money for gas to make the trip. While walking on the street, a man I had never met came up to me and handed me $100. He said, "The Lord told me you need this!"

When I got to Livingston, I again slept in my tent by the river. On Sunday, a guy named Bob came to me and said the Lord told him I was supposed

to live with him. I moved in with him that day.
When the job ended for me, another man moved
in with Bob. He intended to work in sweat pants
and a sweat shirt because he didn't have anything
warmer.

Winter in Montana is brutally cold, with subzero
temps even on a sunny day. I had a pair of
quilted Carhart overalls and coat. The man that
moved in was my size. Since my job was over, I
didn't need them anymore. I gave them to him,
along with my boots and chainsaw.

Scripture says if you have material possessions
you no longer need and see a fellow Christian in
need, you are to give him those possessions.
Then when you have needs, they also will be
met. I guess this goes back to the Parable of the
Sower. Either you believe what the Word
teaches and live it, or you don't.

# Encounter

*Number Seven*

## *A Broken Tractor*

There was a guy named Stan who had worked with me on the job in Livingston. He, along with his wife and children, were trying to buy a ranch and had been doing so for seven months. As part of the stipulation for buying it, they had to prove they could manage it for a year. He was trying to plant his corn crop in time for feeding his cattle, when his tractor seized up and wouldn't start again.

I visited Stan at the ranch the next day, and he told me what happened. He explained there was a man up the trail who had an old tractor for rent. He hoped he might be able to get his crop in using that. He asked if I'd accompany him and his wife to see if they could negotiate a price they could afford. The man wanted so much money to rent the tractor that Stan couldn't afford it. He told his wife, "I guess we just lost the ranch."

I interjected, "No, there is one more thing to do. Let me pray with you about this."

They agreed, so I held their hands and said, "Lord I know that You don't need to do it this way, but if I have any favors coming, let me cash them in. Instead, You help Stan, because he needs Your help."

Stan asked, "That's all?"

"Short, sweet and from the heart," I said. "He knows your heart and doesn't like lengthy prayers!"

Stan called me the next day and said I wasn't going to believe what had happened. I told him at this point in my life, I believed everything that happens. Stan said there was a man driving down the road who saw his tractor out in the field. He knew by looking at it that it wasn't running. The man took Stan to his ranch and brought back his brand-new John Deere tractor with all the attachments to go with it. The other gentleman hadn't even used it yet; it didn't even have five miles on it. With the use of the tractor, Stan would be able to get his corn planted.

I said, "Yep, that's Him. That's His style!"

Stan replied, "But all you did was ask."

I explained, "That's what He says to do; ask and believe it to be so."

# Encounter

*Number Eight*

## *A Garage Sale Violin*

I have been given five spiritual gifts thus far: the gift of tongues, interpretation of tongues, discernment of spirits, the gift of healing, and the gift of faith. I am a U.S. Navy Vietnam veteran. Every time I meet another Vietnam vet, I always tell them, "Welcome home." I do this because we didn't get this when we came home from the war.

In Oklahoma City, Oklahoma, I met a couple, a husband and wife. He was a Vietnam vet. He had metal braces on his legs and metal crutches to help him walk from a battle injury. I shook his hand and told him, "Welcome home," then went back to my place. About ten minutes later, there was a knock on my door. I opened it, and the man's wife was standing in my doorway crying.

I asked her if I could help her. She said, "You're an Angel."

I said, "No ma'am, I'm a human being as far as I know," but she again told me I was an Angel.

I asked her to explain what we were talking about. She said, "You shook my husband's hand, and his braces fell off! He's walking!"

I responded, "Well praise God! I didn't do that, that's not me. I'm the channel, like the messenger boy. It passes through me, but give the glory to God, not me."

While still in Oklahoma City, I went to a real estate office. I was looking to maybe buy a house as that was God's idea for the day. I knew it must have been His idea, because I didn't have any money. I found five houses in their listings I thought I would like to see, but I picked out one in particular. The real estate agent and I went to see it, and as things turned out, it was the only one I looked at.

The woman of the house met us at the door and gave us a tour. It was a magnificent house! We went outside to the patio by the pool. I looked at the woman and said, "You don't really want to sell your house, do you?"

She said no, but her husband had cancer and gambling debts they needed to pay off. She looked at me and asked if I would pray with her; I said I would. I prayed that they wouldn't have to sell the house and that her husband be healed of cancer and gambling (not my will, but God's will be done).  As we walked to the door, the woman said there was one more thing she needed to do that day.  She said her grandchild wanted to learn to play the violin and she needed to shop for one.

**I** told her to wait on her porch, that I'd be right back.  I had been to a yard sale earlier that morning and had bought a violin for $5.  I don't play violin, so I didn't know at the time why I was buying it.  But since I've had similar experiences, I was sure this was just another one, like all the others.  I retrieved the violin from my car and gave it to her.  She exclaimed, "This is a $3,000 violin!"  I told her I only paid $5 at a yard sale, so it was hers.  Such things are common occurrences for me.

**I** saw the woman and her husband three weeks later and asked how things were going.  She said a miracle had happened.  Her husband's cancer was gone, and a man came to them and paid off their gambling debts.

# Encounter

*Number Nine*

## First Fruits of my Labor

If there is one thing, I've failed at in life, it is tithing. I will admit I have tried it. In fact, when I lived in Pelzer, South Carolina, I read in Scripture to bring all the tithes into the storehouse. I asked God where the storehouse was. I was in the grocery store one day, and by the exit I saw collection barrels for food to give to the poor. God said to me, "Here is one of my storehouses."

After that, every time I went grocery shopping, I first shopped for groceries to feed the poor to put in the barrels, and then I would do my own shopping. A year or so later, the barrels were removed. I asked God where the next storehouse was. Even though we're told by churches they are the storehouse, I've never believed that.

But then in Oklahoma City, I went to an all-black church and knew by discernment, the preacher was the real thing. When payday came, I took my tithe and offering directly to the minister. Before a penny was spent on anything, this tithe was to be the very first fruits of my labor. I was so low on gas I wondered if I would have enough to get there, but on faith I waited until after I had given my tithe and offering to get gas. The minister prayed with me over the offering.

That same day, I received what I found out later was the gift of faith. I found myself shouting (and I don't shout a lot) positive affirmations of prosperity on a level I wouldn't even have dreamed thinking. I shouted, "I am a trillionaire and have a 20,000-acre ranch where I raise cattle and buffalo. I am building an orphanage that's so wonderful the children won't want to be adopted; they'll want to make this their home.

"I will hire the best chefs from Le Cordon Bleu Culinary College (where I recently attended and got straight A's) and the best teachers in the world. Children from all over the world will have the best education possible and can become anything they want to in life.

"As part of the staff, I will hire grandfathers, grandmothers, widows, and widowers to help raise the children and pass on their values. When it comes time for their passing, they will have all these children to love and comfort them in their last moments. They won't be in some hole where no one cares about them anymore."

As I spoke those words out loud, I believed with no doubt at that moment these things were real. It was as if I could reach out and actually touch them. I had never believed like that in my entire life! Finally, I was believing, without doubting!

I remember speaking to God in that moment and saying, "I know when you speak of 'mountains' in Scripture, you're probably talking about obstacles in our way. But quite honestly with belief on this level, I know with no doubt if I told Mt. McKinley to move, it would move." That's a big mountain, and that is some strong faith!

Right after that I went to speak with a preacher I know to tell him what had happened. I walked into his office, and he fell out of his chair backwards while his secretary screamed. I looked behind me and asked, "What?"

The preacher said there was an aura all around me. I told them what had just happened. The preacher explained I had just been in the very presence of the Holy Spirit. The gift of faith is different than the faith all Christians have. The gift of faith and the gift of healing go hand in hand, and work together. Jesus said, "These things and more you will do."

# Encounter

*Number Ten*

## *God's Foot on My Truck*

In Montana after the incident with Stan, my Pontiac broke down. I gave it to Stan for his wife. She wanted to drive it in a demolition derby; it was built like a tank, so it was appropriate. I was now without a vehicle, so I told God I needed transportation.

I remember needing to go to town that day. I was walking toward the highway, and a man pulled up and asked if I needed a ride. I told him I needed a ride to town. He was going the opposite direction, but he was willing to take me to town. Town was twenty miles away which means he went forty miles out of his way. When I was ready to return, someone else offered to drive me. Both times, I didn't have my thumb out trying to hitch a ride.

For two weeks that kept happening. I spoke again to God and said, "Okay, so I called You on this and You have a good sense of humor. But I need my own transportation." At the time, someone told me that in asking and praying I needed to be specific.

I found a red and black Chevy K-5 Blazer in the paper in Bozeman, Montana and went to see it. It was a 1985 model and the present year was 1997. It had 32,000 miles on it and the lady was asking $3,200. For that price, she could have sold ten of them in a day. I wanted that truck. I remember thinking at the time it was probably wishful thinking on my part and to forget about it; I only had about $200 to my name.

A month later I saw the woman who owned the truck at the post office in town. She approached me and asked if I still wanted her K-5 Blazer. In astonishment I asked her, "You never sold that truck?"

She said no. They ran ads for a month and drove around with For Sale signs all over it. She explained after I had come to see it, NOBODY else came to see it, nobody called, no one was interested. I said, "Well, God and I are kinda tight, so maybe He has His hand on it for me."

She exclaimed, "I think He has His feet on it, too!"

Three days later a man walked up to me and handed me $3,200 and said, "God said you needed this." I bought the truck with the money. I was also given money for the license plate, insurance and gas. I was then offered a job in Oscoda, Michigan.

I left Montana. I think of all the places in the United States, I like Oregon, Montana, Idaho, Colorado and West Virginia the best. But I've been to every state except Hawaii and have fond memories in each state. God Bless America.

# Selah – A Time to Pause

*I want to say to you, the reader of this, I don't know that I ever asked for all this stuff to happen. My bottom line is, I don't have a bottom line except that one day I'll kneel before Almighty God. I have shared my experiences with God with several people over the years. The resounding response from them has always been that I should write this book for the whole world to read. I trust it will truly help you and strengthen your faith in God and all that He can do. And I hope that you will be willing to be used by Him. You will never regret this choice.*

# Encounter

*Number Eleven*

## *She Witnessed the Light*

I know a woman named Carol in Surprise, Arizona, who claimed to be an atheist. When she told me, I guess I smirked a bit. She said, "What's so funny?"

I said, "Well, it's not funny and I don't want to appear to be arrogant. But if you have anything to do with me and stay an atheist, good luck."

She replied, "He's not going to change me!"

I responded, "What did you just say?"

She answered, "I didn't say anything."

"You just said 'He's not going to change me,'" I replied, "Yet you just acknowledged His presence. It's over and done. You're His."

She said, "Oh, my God."

"Bingo," I said, "Boy, that was quick!"

We went to the gym one day after that encounter. After our workout, we went to use the dry sauna. We were only in for a bit when a guy walked in and sat across from us. He said, "Hi, my name is Bob, and I'm a cocaine addict."

I was thinking, "Wow, who introduces himself like this?"

Carol asked him why he was telling us this. He relayed he'd been to six treatment centers, but that he hadn't been able to kick the habit. I told him, "Well Bob, you're not going to be able to kick the habit on your own, but there is a way."

"Are you trying to tell me about Jesus and God?" he asked.

I told him I was. He said he wasn't sure he was ready for that. I told him he had better get ready, and he better do it right now. I said, "You're in a dry sauna telling a total stranger that you're a coke addict. Who does that? How do you know I'm not a cop?

"Believe me, Bob," I continued, "you are being warned big time. You are standing right at the crossroads. Jesus is on the right and Satan is on the left. Both are offering you their hand. Whose hand do you want to take?

"You haven't kicked the habit," I told him, "and you could overdose tonight. You will then stand before the Almighty, and God will remind you that you were warned.

"Bob, if I were you," I advised, "I'd go tie myself to a tree out in the woods for a week. You are in a very dangerous place, but also in a very good place. Now is the time to decide."

We prayed with Bob, and I hope he made the decision for Christ.

Later, Carol and I went to a car dealer to look at cars. We were sitting talking to a salesman. In the middle of his conversation, he stood up, mid-sentence, didn't excuse himself, didn't say I'll be right back, and left. Carol looked at me and questioned, "What is happening?"

All of a sudden, the owner of the dealership came in and sat in front of us. He began confessing to me what he had done. He said he was ashamed and asked if God would forgive him. Carol asked, "Why is he telling all this to you?" I told her I didn't know.

He finished talking and left the room. The salesman came back and continued his interrupted sentence, as if he had never left. That was weird. All I can figure was he saw the light in me. Other people have mentioned seeing the light in me.

# Encounter

*Number Twelve*

## *Good Morning, General!*

Just over four years ago, I was driving outside Dunreith, Indiana, south and east of Indianapolis. I saw a Victorian-style farmhouse off to my left. In passing, I must have openly said, "Wow, that's a pretty house!" That's when God spoke to me, and when God speaks, it's loud. He told me to turn around and go to the house I was just admiring and ask if it was for sale.

I answered, "Lord, there's not even a 'For Sale' sign in front, and I don't have any money." I continued to drive.

Louder than the first time the Lord said, "Don't argue with me! Do what you are told to do!"

This time I listened and turned around. I rang the doorbell and a little girl came to the door. I inquired if the house was for sale. She told me to wait and called to someone. An older woman came to the door and asked if she could help me. I said, "Ma'am, I don't mean to bother you, but the Lord told me to ask you if your house was for sale.

"**I** tried to explain to Him that you didn't even have a 'For Sale' sign in the front yard," I continued, "but He told me not to argue. So, I'm just doing what I was told."

**S**he asked, "The Lord sent you here?"

**I** told her that He did, and she asked me to come inside the house. We talked for two hours. She was a missionary. I mean seriously, what are the chances? She told me the house wasn't for sale, but it was available. I asked her what she meant by that. She explained the house was built in 1840 and was part of the Underground Railroad in the Civil War. She then asked if I had the house what I would do with it.

**W**hen I was in that house, I felt passion on a level I'd never experienced before. I said, "Ma'am, the first thing that comes to my mind every time I see a place like this is, 'it would make a great retreat!'

"**I**'ve always been told I'm supposed to have a place where people come and can be at peace with God," I told her, "and since it is my God-given talent to cook as well as I can (I can cook better than any gourmet chef), I guess I'd meet their needs as best I could."

She replied, "That's what I did with the house. It's known as 'The Open Door.'"

Her name was Mother Pauline McBride. I told her I didn't know any more that what we had already discussed. We agreed to exchange phone numbers, go our separate ways and pray about it.

Three months later she called and asked, "So, when are you coming?"

I said, "Ma'am, I can't afford your house. It must be a $3-million property." Again, she asked me when I was coming. I said, "Ma'am, even if I sold my little house, I couldn't even afford to make a down payment on your house."

She said, "I'm not selling it to you, I'm giving it to you."

I replied, confused, "You're doing what?"

She explained she was 88 years old and her mission field was in Haiti. I questioned if it was in Port Au Prince, Haiti at the Baptist Mission.

She asked, "How do you know that?" I told her I was there when I was in the Navy.

"This is interesting," she said, "but I have to warn you about something. My ministry is prophesy, so if you come here, you'll die here."

I asked, "Do you mean of old age?"

She replied, "No."

She then told me that sometime in the next five years there would be a civil war here in the United States, and it will involve the Muslims. She said a "stand" will be made at her house. I explained I was told in a dream that I would make a "stand." She asked, "Were you told how many you would stand with?"

I told her in my dream, I will stand with 5,000. She replied that was the exact number she had also seen. She then said, "Let me ask you another question. Has someone recently called you by a name you're not used to being called?"

I told her that three days ago I was at a gun show in Greenville, South Carolina. A muscular-looking man with a physique like Arnold Schwarzenegger used to have walked up to me and said, "Good Morning, General!"

I saluted, chuckled, and asked him what he was talking about because I'm not a General. The man then responded, "You're a five-star General in God's Army."

Mother Pauline said, "He's exactly right."

"But ma'am, I don't know that," I replied.

She told me that I didn't know it yet. She paused for a moment and it was as if I could see her looking off into the distance. She then said she was just told that I do know that. I asked, "Excuse me?"

She answered, "I was just told that you had an experience when you were age twelve. You had the same experience until you were thirty-two. In that 20-year period, it happened over 300 times."

Surprised, I told her that only God and I knew about those experiences. I had never told anyone about it; if I had, they would have thought that I was insane. She asked me to tell her about it. I said, "No, if He just told you about it, then you tell me."

She said, "Okay, you are twelve years old, in the living room of your parent's house. There's an archway between the living room and dining room.  It's a portal.

"You walk through the archway," she continued, "and for five seconds, you're a full-grown adult on the back of a dapple-grey horse.  You have a saber in your hand.  You're in a big green field and there are thousands behind you.

"You look to your left, and you're dressed like everybody else, like the household cavalry of England.  They have silver breast plates on, but only yours is gold.  They have on silver helmets, only your helmet is gold.  All of their horses have white tails hanging down the side, but your horse has a red hair tail hanging down on your right side.

"You don't see this because it hangs to your right and you are looking to the left.  A red tail and gold armor are the sign of a General.  You are leading God's army," she finished.

 That was exactly the experience I had.  I asked when I was supposed to be there and she said, "God will let you know!"

After that I was in Scottsdale, Arizona.  A man came up to me and said, "Good morning,

General." I had never met him before, but he said he was my first lieutenant.

Two Native Americans later told me they were my scouts. Then, another guy asked me if we were supposed to bring guns, and I told him no. He asked, "Aren't we going to fight Muslims?"

I answered, "Well, first of all, I wasn't told to bring guns. Second, the house has always been a place of refuge. And third, if this is God and His Angels, what could stand against you and win? Guns would only provoke something you wouldn't want. Guns would put it in the natural, and this is all supernatural."

# Encounter

*Number Thirteen*

## *Thousands of Angels*

I had a shop in Pendleton, Oregon where I made and sold buckskin clothes. When that episode ended, I was given a job working on planes in San Antonio, Texas as I'm a licensed A&P mechanic. I started on my way to the new job. Traveling down from Sumpter, Oregon towards Baker City, there is a canyon with a river flowing through it. I pulled my Hummer H2 off the side of the road. I unfolded my chair and sat just to enjoy the peace since I was the only person there.

A state trooper pulled in and started walking toward me. I looked at him and asked, "Can I help you officer?"

He said, "Yeah, I saw all you people standing here, and it seemed to be an awful lot of people to be in one place." He said he first thought everybody was fishing, but he now saw that nobody was.

Confused, I asked him, "Would you mind saying that again? As far as I know, you and I are the only two people here."

"Are you pulling my leg?" he asked while chuckling.

I replied, "Are you pulling mine? Did you have too much coffee to drink?"

Now completely sober, He responded, "You really don't see them?"

I said, "Officer, you and I are the only two people here. Can you tell me what it is you're seeing?"

He proceeded to tell me there were thousands of people, and they were all about 14 feet tall! I said, "Officer, I am 6'7" and that's pretty tall. I don't know anybody 14 feet tall."

He looked at me, looked around at "them," and then looked at me again. He slowly walked back to his patrol car, tripping twice, and then drove away slowly. Well, that was different.

# Encounter

*Number Fourteen*

## The Waring Angels

**I** finally made it to Texas. In Laredo, I went into a café to get a bite to eat. I was having a bowl of Famous Texas Chili when a biker came up to me on my left side; he seemed a little hesitant to even speak to me. But he asked, "Are you in the right place?"

**I** told him I just came in to get a bite to eat and would be leaving as soon as I was done. He said, "You're fine, but those guys that came in with you, we're not really happy about them." I asked what he was talking about. He pointed and said, "Those guys over there, the ones that are about 14 feet tall."

**I** didn't see anybody, but I said, "Oh yeah, they'll leave when I do."

**H**e replied, "We don't wanna go near them."

**A**fter that, I called Mother Pauline who owns the house in Dunreith. I asked her, "Mother Pauline, you said that I lead God's Army as one of His

Generals. Are you talking about His Angel Army?"

She answered, "Yes, I believe so." I told her what had been happening and she said, "Yes, those are waring angels."

I understand that Mother Pauline has since passed away. Am I still supposed to be at her house? I don't know, but I suppose God will tell me.

Prior to her passing, she called me and said, "I had a dream about you. You were in armor on the dapple-grey horse with your army behind you. You were carrying a spear-tipped lance with a banner." She explained she couldn't read what was on the banner.

I told her I had the same dream. There were two people in Israel who translated what was written on the banner for me. It read, "One Republic Under God."

Mother Pauline said, "You were in full armor and your army was with you. You were marching on Washington, D.C." I again told her I had the same dream.

# Encounter

*Number Fifteen*

## *In Fellowship with Hell's Angels*

One summer, I was laid off work in Denver, Colorado, due to the oil crunch and the Exxon Shale Oil Project at Shute Creek near Kemmerer, Wyoming. I hadn't had a vacation in a long time, so I jumped in my MGB sports car and took off heading for Nova Scotia, where I was born. On the way my "B" broke down in Kearney, Nebraska.

There was a bike shop that advertised working on MG's, so I pulled in. I was told they couldn't start work on my car for three days because there was a person ahead of me. I explained I wasn't in a big hurry. The owners of the shop asked where I was going to stay. I had seen a campground down the road, so I said I would go there.

They said that was no good and took me to their farm instead. They helped me pitch my tent under a willow tree. While we were setting up camp, a van drove up with a Harley Softail on it. They asked if I knew how to ride. When I said I did, they offered to let me drive the motorcycle while I was in town.

It was the local chapter of Hell's Angels. Every day we all had breakfast, lunch and dinner together. I'd go to the shop and help them polish up bikes and clean up the shop. I had a pet timber wolf at the time, and they loved her.

Finally, my car was fixed, and I got hugs from everyone as I was leaving. One of the members of the group, Denny, said, "It was like Ron was one of us all along!" They made me an honorary member of their chapter.

A guy named Bear came up, gave me a hug and said, "I like you Ron."

I said, "I like you too, Bear."

Another member, Darwin, told me they were glad Bear liked me because he would have killed me if he hadn't.

I left and had driven 500 miles when my oil pressure gage went to zero. I called Darwin and asked what I should do. He and a few others drove the 500 miles and fixed the problem. We had dinner together and we all stayed the night. After more hugs in the morning, I was on my way. They didn't charge me for the repair.

**I** stopped in Pipestone, Minnesota to find out why they called it Pipestone. As it turns out, it was a place on the Great Lakes where the Indians got the red stone for their peace pipes. I ended up buying three long-stem peace pipes. I sent one back to Darwin and the boys. Darwin called me and said, "Yeah, it's been really peaceful around here lately! We've been smoking all kinds of stuff in the pipe you sent!"

**I** replied, "I kinda thought you would."

# Encounter

*Number Sixteen*

## God Cares About What's Lost

I made it to Halifax, Nova Scotia. At the end of the summer, the crew of the Blue Nose II Schooner were having a party on McNabs Island. My date and I brought some lobsters and had a grand time. She was carrying my wallet for me in her jeans pocket, and sometime during the evening she needed to use the bathroom. Since we were outside, she went off by herself and took care of business. In doing so, she apparently dropped my wallet.

We didn't realize until we got back to Halifax that it was lost. The next day, I went to look for my wallet. I searched for five hours and got to the point where I said, "Okay, it's gone, I accept it." I then looked up to God and said, "Give me a break! I now have to get new ID's and a new passport to be able to get back into the United States."

For no reason, I looked over my right shoulder. I turned and walked in that direction, and within 25 yards I stepped right on my wallet.

Everything was still in it, even the money! I fell to my knees pretty quickly and praised God.

Two weeks later, I met a man named Chris Oland, who owned Oland Breweries. Chris let me use one of his Harleys to tour the Maritimes. I was out driving when I came upon a group of young people who looked like they had lost something. They were all searching in a big, open wheat field.

I stopped in the road and asked the closest person to me what was going on. I was told a young girl had lost her engagement ring. She had been showing her new ring to her friends and placed it on the hood of a truck so they could see the sunlight refracting in the diamond. The truck jumped and the ring went flying into the wheat field. A gold-banded diamond ring in a golden wheat field – a proverbial needle in a hay stack!

I parked the bike, walked to the other side of the road and said, "Lord, I know what is going on here. This is just like my wallet again." I went to the young girl and asked if she was a Christian. She said yes. I told her since they had been looking for three hours, she should just let go and ask God to help her.

I walked back to the other side of the road to get back on my bike. I told the Lord, "I don't even want to be the hero here. Let her find her own ring."

It was about two minutes later that she screamed, "I found it! I found it!" She ran over to me with big tears in her eyes and said, "I just let go and asked God to help. And it was sitting on the golden head of a wheat stalk!"

The next episode was lost keys. I was working at Lockheed Martin, and at the end of the day one of my team members had lost his keys. We searched for his keys for several hours. I then told him about the other experiences and advised him to let go and ask God to help.

I heard a voice that said, "Look on the desk." There was a desk, so I looked on and inside the desk. There were no keys. The voice again said to look on the desk. There was an enclosed office with a desk inside. And there were the keys, sitting right on top!

# Encounter

*Number Seventeen*

## A Little Girl's Prayer

The next time I had an experience with lost keys, I had gone to a ranch to ride my Tennessee Walker [horse]. There was a little girl I had never seen before, and she was moping around. I asked if she was going to be riding. She told me she and her parents had already ridden. While riding, they had dropped their car keys and were now out looking for them. It was autumn and leaves littered the trail.

I asked, "How about we go looking for them?" She agreed. We took a few steps and I stopped. I told her about the other times this had happened. I said, "How about you pray, then I'll pray, and then we will look. I know God loves to hear a little girl's prayers."

We both prayed and began to look. I had taken three steps when I noticed a flash of light coming out of a pile of leaves. I reached into the pile up to my elbow and pulled out a set of keys. When her parents came back crying, the little girls ran to them shouting that we had found the keys.

She told her parents how it happened. They all praised God.

# Encounter

*Number Eighteen*

## *Jeep Angels*

I was driving from Boulder, Colorado to Denver in my Jeep CJ-7 to get new brakes put on. On the way home after getting the new brakes, there was a clicking noise. I called the shop. A man answered and explained they were closed for the day, but to bring it back in the morning. They would take care of it then, but it was nothing to worry about.

The next morning, I drove to Denver and sat in the waiting room of the shop. The manager rushed in with his eyes bulging out of his head. He quickly explained, "We tried to call you before you left home. Our mechanic told us this morning he had been called away while working on your brakes yesterday." He continued, "He was distracted and didn't tighten any of your lug bolts!"

He asked me to come into the shop with him. They had my jeep on the lift, and all my wheels were right where they should be. But there were no lug bolts on any of the wheels! He said to me in bewilderment, "You must have had absolute angels holding those wheels on!"

Later in January, I was on my way to Colorado Springs. I was driving in the slow lane and hit a patch of black ice. My jeep spun across all four lanes, across the center divider into oncoming traffic, across all four of those lanes, before coming to rest on the opposite shoulder. It did all of this without getting hit!

When I got my wits about me, I got back on Highway 25, took the off ramp and tried it again. Again, I spun across all eight lanes to the shoulder without getting hit. I didn't try a third time. I just went home instead.

# Encounter

*Number Nineteen*

## *Obedience is Better than Sacrifice*

My older sister and younger brother live in Boulder, Colorado. I lived there for a short while in a homeless shelter. Yes, I know two of my siblings lived there and might have let me use their garage, basement or backyard. However, my older sister once wrote me a letter telling me I was not welcome in her home. There was no deserved reason that I knew of, and in the same letter she wrote, "You have to understand, Ronnie, that God is a fantasy and money is reality." She had it backwards, but that's her choice. She denies having ever written that letter, but I still have it.

While in Boulder, I was praying about finding work. Before I went to sleep one night, the Holy Spirit came over me. I turned on the light and starting writing down what was coming to my mind. The next night I went to hear a preacher speak, and he spoke on the very same subject. That's confirmation.

After his talk, I met with the preacher and told him what had happened to me the night before.

He asked me what I was told. I explained I was told to work for free, to just do the work and know that I'd be taken care of. I was told by the Holy Spirit to have faith.

It was a Friday, and as the day wore on, I knew what to do. I put an ad in the local paper saying, "I'll do any job, large or small. You provide the materials, and I'll provide the labor at no cost to you." I figured if my needs were met, then I didn't have to earn a wage.

Monday morning, I got up early, around 7:00 a.m. I said, "Well Lord, I've done what you've asked for. The ad is in the paper this morning. I'm kind of new at this concept, but let's have it." As soon as I said, "Let's have it," the phone on the wall rang. I jumped because I was standing right next to the phone.

There was an old man on the phone. He told me he and his wife were an older couple, couldn't do much for themselves anymore, but they needed their house painted. I said I could do that for him. He replied, "We read your ad, but it was worded kind of strangely. What do you charge?"

I said, "Nothing!"

"What do you mean, nothing?" he asked.

I told him nothing, as in no money. He commented I couldn't do that, and I told him that's what I used to think, but now I knew differently. He said, "You can't make a living doing that."

When I explained to him why I wasn't charging money he said, "I'm going to let you work for me, but I'm not going to let you work for nothing!" I told him that was his choice, but I was going to work for nothing. If he gave me a blessing for doing the work, then that was his business.

It was interesting, because when you're working for nothing, you're not thinking all day about how much you're being paid. That's gone. You're not in a big hurry to get to the next job where you're also going to work for nothing; you may as well work here for nothing as work there for nothing. I was literally smiling, singing and laughing all day.

The older gentleman came out five or six times each day to bring me drinks and treats. He made me lunch and dinner every day, telling me to slow down and take breaks. And at the end of five days, he paid me $25 per hour. If I had been charging, I might have asked for $5 an hour.

After that, I got tons of work. Even though I didn't charge, nobody allowed me to work without paying me. In fact, every single person overpaid me!

I was then told by God to get ready for a journey. I was to ride on horseback from where I was in Colorado to Idaho and Montana and to continue doing this kind of work. I told God I had fourteen years' experience riding and caring for horses, so that was not a problem. I didn't have a horse though, and that could be a problem. I would need a good endurance horse, and I sure didn't have the money to buy an endurance horse. I said, "God, you created them. You know what good horse flesh is, so You pick him out."

God asked me, "Are you all packed and ready to go?"

I said, "No Sir, not yet!"

I gave away everything I couldn't take with me. Three days later a Mercedes Benz dealer named Karl called me from his dealership in Longmont, Colorado. He had gotten my phone number, but I don't know how. He questioned, "Do you own a little yellow Spitfire sports car?" I told him I did, and he asked me if I would consider trading it for something.

I asked him, "Trade for what?"

"For two horses," he answered.

One was a Morgan crossed with a thoroughbred horse and the other was an Arabian. Both were endurance horses, were papered and had lineage back to Arabia. I asked Karl why he was willing to trade a $300 car for $30,000 worth of horses. He told me his side of the story, which involved God. As I shared with him my story, it all made sense.

At the same time, I met an all-around cowboy named Orin Bradley. His mother offered to let me keep my horses in her pasture. They also told me I could use the line shack at their place to sleep in until I went on this ride.

I had a list of supplies I would need for my trip. I prayed about this for two weeks, and for two weeks I didn't hear anything from the Lord. So, on a Saturday, I bought my first lottery ticket. The human part of me said, "I know what I'll do, I'll buy a lottery ticket, win the lottery and use the money to buy supplies along the way."

I purchased a Quick Pick lottery ticket and stuck it in my wallet. I went to church the next morning. My home church was Second Baptist Church Boulder. Rev. Hansford Vann was the

Pastor, and my best friend, Bruce Randolph Jr. was there. Bruce's father was Daddy Bruce of Denver.

The sermon that morning was titled, *Trust in God.* Rev. Vann said, "I bet that a bunch of you went out and bought lottery tickets yesterday. You've already seen that you didn't win and already thrown the tickets away."

I sat there thinking, of all the Sundays to bring up this topic it was the week I bought a Quick Pick. I didn't know what numbers were on the ticket (I hadn't looked yet), so I decided I'd check it out after church service. But after running that through my mind, the Lord spoke up and said, "For the last two weeks, you've prayed up a heck of a storm. You have my attention, but like the pastor said, 'Do you trust me, or don't you?'"

I was literally in tears, pulled out the ticket and crumbled it up; I planned to throw it away. The Lord spoke again and said, "Don't throw it away. Put it in the offering envelope and give it to the pastor after the service."

I did just that and handed it to Rev. Vann. I said to him, "The Lord told me that you'd know what to do with this." To this day, I don't know if it was a winning ticket.

The next day I went to the post office to pick up my mail. There was a check for $500 from my sister, the same one whose home I am not welcome in. I put the check and the envelope in my Bible. I took off on foot to go to the bank to cash it. It was a really windy day. While walking to the bank, I was thinking about what I could have to eat; I hadn't eaten in about three days. On the way, I stopped at a tack shop where I had put some shirts for sale that I had made. They were closed.

When I reached the bank, I looked in my Bible for the check, but it was gone. The envelope was still there, but I couldn't find the check. I frantically looked through every page. I dumped the Bible upside down and shook it, but the check wasn't there. I started backtracking all my steps back to the post office, although I assumed it would have blown away if I had dropped it. I knew the postmaster and knew he would let me use his phone. I planned to call my sister and have her cancel payment on the check and resend a new one. I'd get it another day and just starve until then.

I saw the postmaster and he asked how my day was going. I said he didn't want to know, and he replied he wouldn't have asked if he didn't want to know. I told him what had happened, and he said, "Let me see your Bible." I handed it to him, but my mind was in another place. All of a sudden, he pulled out the check and said, "Here it is."

I was floored! "What do you mean, 'Here it is?'" I asked. "I looked through every page and it was not in there."

He answered, "Sometimes things disappear in this book between one page."

"You mean two pages," I said.

He replied, "No, not in this book."

When I put the check back in my Bible this time, I left it sticking out a little so I wouldn't lose it. On my way back to the bank, I stopped again at the tack shop. This time they were open. The owners of the shop, a husband and wife, said they hadn't sold any of my shirts, but they had a proposition for me. They had seen some of the houses I had painted and thought I did excellent work; they asked if I would paint their house, barn and outbuildings.

I told them I would. They said they couldn't pay me in money but asked if I would accept something else instead. They then proceeded to name my entire list of supplies I needed for my trip in the order I had written them. Only God and I knew what was on that list! I was overwhelmed and in tears of joy.

That night as I was approaching the line shack, it was moonless and pitch black. I felt an extremely hostile, evil presence that sent shivers down my spine. I stopped and prayed, and it went away. As I lay down on my cot to go to sleep, someone started banging on the door. A man was yelling that I had to get out of there right now! He helped me load my belongings in his van and we quickly left the area, tires screaming.

As we drove, he apologized for being so demanding and abrupt. He explained he was a Christian minister, and his ministry was to teach Christians about the opposing forces. He said whatever Christians pray for, Satanists pray against it. He told me he follows the activities of the local satanic covens, and I was on their agenda that night; they were going to abduct me, take me to their altar, and kill me. I told him about feeling the evil presence earlier. He said he would have expected that, everything considered.

The minister took me to his house and offered to let me stay with him. He told me he knew I must be doing something awesome because of all the activity going on.  I explained to him what I was doing and how it all came to be.  He said it all made sense now.

The next morning, we were in front of his house. I noticed a white limousine parked down the street facing our way with VIP plates on the front bumper.  I remember saying, "Wow, there's a very important person."

He turned whiter than a ghost and told me it belonged to the high priestess of a local satanic coven.  He said, "You are bringing out the leaders on this."

Later that morning, I had gone to the store and was driving my VW Bug out of the parking lot.  I was sitting on the apron, waiting for a chance to pull out into traffic, when a car pulled up next to me and stopped.  I wondered what the driver was doing stopping there because I knew the stop sign was about five car lengths behind me.  I started to turn to look at him and an angel stepped off my right shoulder and said, "I'll take this."  Our eyes never actually met.  I audibly heard what sounded like swords clashing.

I pulled out and parked back in the lot still watching the car.  I got out of my car and ran to a friend's shop.  I told him what had just happened.

The car was still there, so I pointed it out to my friend. He told me the driver was Antoine Levey, the founder of the Church of Satan.

Later that day, I told the minister what had happened. He said Levey had come to curse me and stop me from doing my ride. He explained the angel blocked the curse. He told me that for me to have audibly heard the sound of swords clashing was significant, but he didn't explain why.

The minister was a professional painter (no coincidence), and together we prayed for five days of sunshine and warm weather as winter was setting in. Warm weather wasn't in the forecast, but we got it anyway. The minister and I started painting the barn and outbuildings of the tack shop owners. He showed me how to prep and paint using his equipment. On the third day, he told me he would join me later and to go ahead and start without him. (*I wonder why the number three is so dominant.)

I set up the equipment and was getting ready to spray when a yellow jacket wasp headed right for my face. I shot it out of the air with paint from my spray gun. A second one came at me, then a third, and I shot both of them out of the air, too. I must have lost consciousness then. When I was conscious again, I counted over 3,000 hornets covered in paint on the ground, but I knew I didn't do it. Then a voice said, "Get out of here. Flee!"

I quickly put all the equipment away. When I was walking to my car, I saw thousands of hornets hovering above me about five stories up. I got in the car and drove away. Right away I told God, "I don't like hornets."

He said, "Did you notice none of them touched you?"

I replied, "Yeah, that's pretty awesome that none of them touched me! But then I remembered Psalm 91."

I told the minister what happened. "Satan knows what in nature you don't like," he said, "but for Satan to be able to pierce into that realm and use something in nature against you, he has to lose something."

I was told the start date for the ride and what trail to take. When the day arrived, a guy named Howard took my horse and myself in his trailer to the starting point and dropped us off; I only took the Morgan as I had sold the Arabian. I was all alone staring at the Rocky Mountains covered in snow. I prayed, "God, you've asked me to do this and I'm on my way. I've always been real with you and you've always been real with me.

"And being real right now is being scared of crossing the Rockies," I continued. "This is wintertime, and it's common knowledge you don't cross the Rockies in the winter on a horse." I said, "Lord, I know who you are. I know it can be summer every step of the way, but I'm still scared."

I was leading my horse on foot to get her used to the extra weight she was carrying. Taking that first step, it felt like my feet weighed so much, it was hard to lift them. But as I walked for a while, it got easier. I had only walked about thirty steps and all of a sudden, my Morgan reared up like she was afraid of something. The next thing I knew, she was down on her knees hiding her head like she was scared of something.

She dumped my gear all over the trail and all of a sudden, she was torn up by barbed wire. I don't know where the barbed wire came from. She was bleeding badly, and I tried to stop the bleeding with some camphor I had. Without warning, an old man said, "Do you need some help?"

I turned and there was an old guy. I don't know where he came from because you could see three miles in every direction, and he wasn't there before just then. My emotions were getting to me and I was shaky. I said, "Yeah, she's torn up pretty badly. I'll need some sutures for her."

He said, "I know where a vet is. I'll go get him."

I turned back around to compress one of the wounds. Out of nowhere, I heard a woman's voice say, "Do you need some help?" I quickly turned around and the old guy was gone, but there were now two women standing there instead. My emotions were all over the place. I'm sure I was crying because I didn't know where these people were coming from.

I said, "Yes, maybe if one of you will hold her, I can get some of the gear up off the trail." One of them explained that when the doctor came back, we could take the horse to a ranch down the trail to take care of her. I started to ask, "Wait a minute, how do you know there's a doctor coming?" However, I didn't even get the words out of my mouth before the guy who had dropped us off drove up with his trailer.

I questioned, "Howard, what are you doing here?" He told me he was called by God to come back and get me. I asked him how far down the road he was before that happened, and he said about twenty miles. I said in bewilderment,

"Howard, this just happened. You were turned around before it even happened."

The doctor came a few minutes later, but he wasn't accompanied by the old guy or the two women; the two women had disappeared while I was talking to Howard, and the old guy never returned. My horse was taken to a private facility. All the bills were paid for, but I don't know by whom.

Howard and I started the drive back to Boulder. I sat there quietly, still in a daze. After several minutes, I finally asked, "Howard, what happened back there?"

He answered, "This has been the most fantastic day of your entire life. God asked you to go do something, and when you obeyed, He stopped you.

"Your horse isn't going anywhere for at least seven months," he continued, "but you went out and did something today that NOBODY would have done. You were tested today, and you passed with flying colors. The angels are partying in heaven.

"It was no different with you and God today as it was between Abraham and God. You obeyed

Him and He stopped you." He finished by saying, "You could have lost your life out there."

I simply replied, "Yeah, but if He's taken you from where He's taken me and brought you to where He's brought me, you owe Him that much."

On Sunday, I told my friend, Bruce Randolph Jr., what had happened. He quoted the passage in Scripture about Balaam and Balak, the donkey, and the Angel with the flaming sword. Bruce said, "Now I'm not saying you had an Angel in your path with a flaming sword, but your horse was afraid of and trying to hide from something. And the million-dollar question is still, 'Who were those people, the old guy and the two women, and who paid all your bills?'"

I answered in a question, "Angels?"

Bruce said, "Yes."


**A note:** How did Howard know where I was if this wasn't real?

# Encounter

*Number Twenty*

## *Swahili Keys*

Next, I was in Scottsdale, Arizona. I was leaving a Fry's Grocery Store, and I heard a black woman behind me. She was ranting and raving on her cell phone in a language I'd never heard before. I turned to face her and asked if she was speaking Swahili. She said, "Yes, do you speak Swahili?"

I told her, "I have never heard it before. But not only do I know it's Swahili, I know what you said in English." She asked me to interpret. I said, "You've lost your car keys and you've been looking for three hours. Your groceries are melting, and you don't know how you are going to get home." She said that was exactly what she had said.

I said, "Now we will find your keys."

She asked, "But, how?"

I told her to stand by her car, let go and ask God to help. She did so, then asked me what to do next.  I said, "We just wait for what happens next."

I then heard a voice say, "Look in the bush." There was a bush behind me.  I reached in and pulled out a set of keys!

# Conclusion:

Let me say that I don't mean to make enemies of the various religions. In Scripture, God does say to not forbid the coming together of people to pray for the common good in order to praise and honor God. There is mention in Scripture that no food is unclean; all food is good, but some people only have enough faith to eat some of the food, while some can eat all of it. All things are permissible, but not all things are beneficial. Life is a series of choices and consequences. You make a choice, and you must accept the consequence that goes with it.

Do I propose that I have all the answers? NO! Do I have some of the answers? Maybe, but that's not for me to decide. All I intended to do here was share with you what I've experienced in life and in putting into practice what I have learned in living the wisdom and knowledge I have found in the Word and by God's leading.

Either you really believe "the Word" of God and live it, or you don't. If you don't, you are just wasting your time. You can't fool God as He knows your heart. Of the nine gifts of the Holy Spirit, I have been given five gifts so far: the gift of tongues, the gift of interpretation of tongues, the gift of discernment, the gift of healing, and the gift of faith.

I don't have a doctorate in theology; I'm merely chosen by God and willing to be used by Him. The bottom line and all that is important to me is that one day I will be judged and hear the Lord God Almighty say, "Welcome home my good and faithful servant."

About eight months ago, I was living in Thermopolis, Wyoming. At 5:00am one morning, I was abruptly awakened by the sound of a blaring trumpet. I got out of bed, turned on the lights, and looked outside the window. There was no one there. I walked around my apartment, and again there was no one there.

I then heard a man's voice audibly say, "Are you ready?"

I thought for a moment and answered, "Yes, I'm ready!"

"But," I started to say, only I didn't get an opportunity to continue. He answered the thought I had in my mind before I could speak it. Satan can't read your mind, so this messenger had to be from the Heavenly Realm.

What I was about to say was, "But, if my name is not written in the Lamb's Book of Life, then I'm not ready!"

Before I could say this out loud, He said, "Would I be speaking to you if it wasn't?"

At that moment I knew my name is written in the Lamb's Book of Life. That's everything!!

You could be the poorest person on the face of this earth, and you are still one of the richest! You could own the entire universe if that was possible, and it would pale in comparison! To me the ultimate bottom line is that one day you'll kneel before God Almighty and if He isn't saying, "Welcome home," good luck!

Which do you prefer, smoking or non-smoking?

Hell was not created for man.

# My Christmas Poem

When I was a child, I often would hear of Santa, his sleigh and 8 tiny reindeer. Of candy and toys, a gift-wrapped surprise, and bright colored lights that would open your eyes.

But these days I wonder if the whole world forgot, just why it is that we celebrate a lot.

One day every year and each time the same 25th of December and who is to blame, for making this Holiest Day a real shame.

Santa's not real and neither is his sleigh, but Jesus Christ is, and this is His Birthday.

This time we need to put our foot down and tear this old Santa thing down to the ground.

It's filled us with hate, contempt and bad manners, and sometimes I wonder just who the planners.

The ones who are trying to fill us with woe, the ones who would kill us and laugh as we go.

The challenge is love and not all this hate, this time we need Satan's head on a plate.

So, share with your neighbor, a small gift or token, of love and this chain of hate will be broken.

Then we can rest and be rid of our plight, Merry Christmas to all and to all a good night.

# Closing:

In all my years of travelling around this and other countries, I'd always see towns where people settled down. I have often wondered why they picked this spot over another. But today, the 2nd of January 2017, I was going north out of Dillon, Montana and came to a place called Silver Star. It's not even a town, but I know that's the place for me.

If you buy my book and enjoy reading it, and if what I've witnessed with God has strengthened your faith, then you'll be closer to God and I'll finally have the log and stone home I've always wanted. If my 94-year-old mother is still alive, she will come to live with me.

If my book sells really well, I'll fulfill another promise to God and build an orphanage that is so wonderful, the children will not want to be adopted. I'll hire the very best Le Cordon Bleu chefs and the best teachers so the children can become whatever they want to be in life. I'll hire grandfathers and grandmothers, along with widows and widowers who love children to help raise them and pass on their traditions and values. When it comes their time to pass on, there will be hundreds of children who will love them and comfort them in their last moments instead of being off in some hole where no one cares about them anymore.

It will be called "The Master's Touch," and the cycle will continue as I set it up as a trust after I too pass on.

When you buy a copy of my book, I'll want your name to add to the honor roll to show those who helped make the orphanage a reality.

If you want to be on the honor roll of having been builders of The Master's Touch Orphanage and have your name on a brick, here is my email address to send me your name.

ronalddempsey@yahoo.com

Made in the USA
Columbia, SC
25 October 2020